P9-EMB-694

The education system is under pressure today to give up its reliance on tradition and the accepted goals of the past. Educators are challenged on every front to improve abilities, redefine purposes and maintain relevant aims that best serve both student and community. There are sober pleas to humanize education and increasing insistence that every educator subscribe to selfevaluation schedules.

This new book confronts current topics of interest to teacher, principal, and curriculum specialist. It offers a unique self-instructional format that permits the reader to select programs desired, provides practice along with knowledge, and includes mastery test for each program discussed.

The book explores the design and use of instructional objectives. Its practical approach covers how to decide on important goals, how to design instruments to measure those goals, the relationships of objectives and the humanistic movement, and how to develop objectives in the critical area of attitudes.

*Expanding
Dimensions
of
Instructional
Objectives*

Expanding Dimensions of Instructional Objectives

Eva L. Baker

W. James Popham

Graduate School of Education

University of California, Los Angeles

PRENTICE-HALL, INC.
Englewood Cliffs, New Jersey

Library of Congress Cataloging in Publication Data

BAKER, EVA L

   Expanding dimensions of instructional objectives.

     1. Curriculum planning. 2. Behaviorism (Psychology)
     3. Educational tests and measurements. I. Popham,
W. James, joint author. II. Title.

LB1570.B32   371.3   72–8894
ISBN 0–13–294868–0
ISBN 0–13–294850–8 (pbk.)

© **1973 by Prentice-Hall, Inc.**
Englewood Cliffs, N.J.

10 9 8 7 6 5 4 3 2 1

Printed in the United States of America

Prentice-Hall International, Inc., *London*
Prentice-Hall of Australia, Pty. Ltd., *Sydney*
Prentice-Hall of Canada, Ltd., *Toronto*
Prentice-Hall of India Private Limited, *New Delhi*
Prentice-Hall of Japan, Inc., *Tokyo*

Contents

v

Companion Audiovisual Materials

A set of filmstrip-tape instructional programs coordinated with the contents of this book is available from Vimcet Associates Inc., P.O. Box 24714, Los Angeles, California, 90024. Information regarding these materials is available upon request.

*Expanding
Dimensions
of
Instructional
Objectives*

Introduction

The topic of instructional objectives has stimulated much thought and more discussion in the last five years. This book of programs attempts to treat some of the central problems of the use of instructional objectives. The first program, "Humanizing Educational Objectives," was written to demonstrate that the tenets of humanism and behaviorism may have a point of tangency. The program is designed to stimulate the reader to explore alternative ways of using objectives in classroom situations. Involving students in the selection of objectives is one way to help objectives meet individual needs. A step-by-step procedure for determining objectives based on the contribution of relevant groups (students, parents, experts, futurists, etc.) is included in "Deciding on Defensible Goals via Educational Needs Assessment." Another difficult area in the formulation of objectives is the identification of objectives which measure students' attitudes and interests. "Identifying Affective Objectives" presents an approach which should prove helpful in this regard. The final two programs focus on practical matters of writing reasonably good objectives. "Defining Content for Objectives" urges

1

the user to beware of test-item equivalent objectives that can easily lead to rote learning situations. "Writing Tests Which Measure Objectives" presents a view that objectives should *never* be constructed without test items or measurement. A procedure to guide the construction of items relevant to objectives is described in this program.

Organization of the Book

A more detailed description of each program is offered below:

HUMANIZING EDUCATIONAL OBJECTIVES. This program attempts to demonstrate that instructional technology can have positive impact in classrooms. Examples are provided in which measurable objectives are formulated for social and personal development goals. Procedures for systematically involving individual learners in the selection of their unique objectives are also described.

DECIDING ON DEFENSIBLE GOALS VIA EDUCATIONAL NEEDS ASSESSMENT. This program examines a strategy for systematically securing the preferences of various representative groups in order to establish educational goals. After completing the program the reader will be able to design a plan for an educational needs assessment procedure which incorporates the technical procedures described in the program.

IDENTIFYING AFFECTIVE OBJECTIVES. Perhaps the most difficult task of those who must formulate objectives is the generation of noncognitive, that is, affective objectives. This program provides a four-step strategy for designing affective objectives and gives the reader practice in using the strategy.

DEFINING CONTENT FOR OBJECTIVES. In this program the application of behavioral objectives is made feasible in an ordinary classroom situation. Teachers are taught that operational objectives should specify content that is generalizable beyond a single test item. The student learns to identify objectives which do and do not exemplify content generality and to write objectives which do.

WRITING TESTS WHICH MEASURE OBJECTIVES. Because standardized measures are often not appropriate for objective-based instruction, the use of the "item form" approach to writing testing situations is described. Practice is given in transforming objectives into this format and producing items which match objectives.

Use of the Book

Since these programs are self-instructional, it is probable that you will proceed individually through each at your own pace. Incidentally, it is usually better to complete a whole program at a single sitting rather than to interrupt your work. Before commencing a particular program, first locate the answer sheet for that program (and detach it from the book if you wish). Then note the program's objectives and begin reading the textual material. On the answer sheet, write your responses to questions posed in frames. After you have made the response, check the accuracy of your answer by reading further in the program. Preferably, you should respond in writing, although if you wish you may answer mentally. So that you do not inadvertently read too far and see the correct answer before making your response, wide bars like the one below have been inserted throughout the program.

The correct answers will appear immediately following the bar. When you see such a bar, mask off the section below it until you have made your response (a heavy answer mask has been provided inside the rear cover), then *read on to discover the accuracy of your answer.* When you have completed a program, take the mastery test for that program and subsequently check your answers.

Several of the topics treated in these five programs are examined in more detail in the conventional nonprogrammed text, *Systematic Instruction,* distributed by Prentice-Hall, Inc. Also

4

available are related collections of self-instruction programs including *Planning an Instructional Sequence, Establishing Instructional Goals, Evaluating Instruction,* and *Classroom Instructional Tactics.*

Humanizing Educational Objectives

Objectives

This program is designed to counteract arguments that the use of objectives necessarily implies mechanism and memorization. The program attempts to point out ways in which the use of objectives can be turned to "humanistic" purposes through modifying the substances of the objectives, the way they are generated, and the manner in which they are implemented. Specifically, following the reading of the program, the learner should be able to:

1. Generate an objective which deals with process as opposed to more traditional forms of content.
2. Briefly describe a needs-assessment procedure which involves the students as primary sources of objectives.
3. Describe two different ways of implementing objectives.

It may appear to be contradictory that a message of humanism is transmitted through technological means. An instructional program is a form of technology. This program will attempt to provide information to allow you to use elements of instructional technology for the good of people in school. Along the way, you may learn how to better employ one particularly prominent technological artifact to promote humanistic ends.

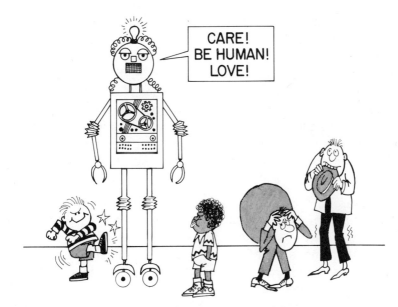

The term "technology" augers the evils of electrodes, dials, and plumbing to many people. Recently, because of unanticipated side effects such as water and air pollution, technology as an endeavor is even less well loved by many people, primarily because early claims made in its behalf were so exalted. A generalized suspicion of science and technology has developed among some groups, which universally indite all varieties of technological advance.

Educational technology has been viewed with heightened skepticism, because its potential is not well understood and fear of its misapplication is especially strong.

The primary message of this section is that most technological artifacts are essentially neutral. The very existence of a technology assures some use of it. Educational technology can be put to good or poor use. You have to decide if you wish to be represented at the time the choice is made.

In this an extended illustration will be used. We are going to focus on one prominent, and thus feared, technological artifact in education—"behavioral objectives" (even the words lack euphony). Measurable instructional objectives are advocated by many because they seem to be able to make teaching more rational and systematic. If teaching is conceived of as an art form, then only those blessed with talent can be good teachers. There is growing evidence that teaching skill can be transmitted to others and that some of these skills bear close relationship to the manner in which students learn.

Critics argue that objectives unduly constrain students and teachers from engaging in spontaneous and satisfying encounters. They also argue the importance of the *process* rather than the *ends* of learning. To give substance to their arguments, they illustrate them with villain objectives such as "The student will name the author of *The Deerslayer*" (a frightening objective on a number of counts), or "He will list the names of the original thirteen colonies with only one error allowed." It is foolish to say that the present state of American education is the fault of disinterested or malicious teachers. It is similarly foolish to assume that freedom from objectives will dramatically change the habits of many experienced teachers. People who have been working in the area of objectives can take account of some of the criticisms directed toward objectives. Moreover, they feel that the formulation and evaluation of certain goals is one of the only ways that desired changes will occur in classrooms.

Many educators and parents think that if operational statements of instructional objectives are prepared, the children are likely to be processed rather than taught, that they will

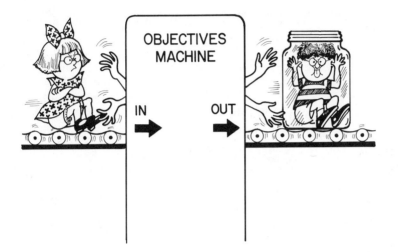

emerge with prestamped and packaged information. The image of an entire generation of people so trained appalls each of us. These fears are amply fed by legislative trends; in state after state, mandates have been issued to use instructional objectives as measures against which to evaluate the effectiveness of school programs in a cost-efficiency model. The idea of evaluation clearly should be supported; unfortunately, its hasty implementation may result in the imposition of objectives which are not easily justified.

The approach taken in this program is that objectives can be one procedure to help you greatly improve your instruction. They can provide benchmarks against which you can personally evaluate your teaching performance. They can inform your students of the goals which they are expected to learn. They can help you add to the curriculum areas and concerns which previously were imperfectly perceived.

How are these mysteries to take place? The first step is to understand *why* objectives were developed and to employ them for the purpose for which they were originally prepared. Objectives should help the designers of instruction plan their activities so that learning is effective and enjoyable. Objectives should also provide a clear basis for determining if desired learning has occurred, for the use of standardized achievement tests does not provide detailed-enough information to permit the teacher to make revisions to improve instructional plans.

Clearly, there is no implication that every classroom activity needs an instructional objective to justify its existence. Rather, only those areas which meet two critical criteria probably need to be operationalized:

1. *The area represents a critical learning which must be included in the school program.*
2. *Means for evaluating the objective can be developed.*

Thus, one class of objectives is instantly eliminated by the application of the first criterion: objectives that are trivial. The memorization of isolated facts phrased as objectives cannot possibly survive the first criterion, for to demonstrate that such behaviors are essential to *anything* is a near hopeless task. Another set of objectives is excluded by application of the second criterion. Global, long-range goals would not be included since the procedures for evaluating them are difficult, if not currently impossible, to implement. For instance, a goal which stated that the learner would make careful decisions regarding the choice of political leaders is probably one which cannot be adequately measured without the violation of privacy of the polling booth.

What is left for the objectives-writers to objectify? If we wipe out the trivial objectives with one stroke and the important and long-range objectives with another, what is left? A careful appraisal of the remaining areas in school programs is very encouraging. The abilities to read, to compute, to reason, to analyze, to write, and really to think remain to be taught. The skills one needs to interact with others, to respect others' positions, values, and expressions while maintaining self-respect are still left. And many more. The areas mentioned represent those which meet both criteria. First, they are probably essential for any serious school program and they can be adequately measured. In addition, many of them can be taught in many different subject matter organizations.

If we can tentatively agree, then, that there are some worthwhile areas which might be converted to operational statements of instructional intentions, that is, fancy language for instructional objectives, then we can move on to the process of "humanizing" them and making them more suitable for a school rather than a factory.

How does one begin the process of humanizing the goals of instruction? There are three main ways to proceed.

We can (1) change the substance of the objectives so that they represent concern for the individual, (2) apply procedures for developing objectives so that individuals have more to say about what they will learn, and (3) improve the way objectives are implemented. The first two general procedures will be of major concern here, and the third will be lightly touched on.

If we begin the process of humanizing objectives, we must consider the substance of the instructional goals themselves. One widely proclaimed tenet of humanism is that it is the *process* of life rather than its end accomplishments which are worthwhile. If we accept the importance of process, then a valuable source for instructional objectives becomes available to us, for what we wish to improve is the process by which students are learning. We hope that they are stimulated by the entire learning experience rather than simply proud of the final outcome, such as a good grade on an examination.

How can process be measured and how can we formulate sensible statements of it? Suppose you were faced with the following situation.

By Number 1 on your answer sheet sketch out a process-type objective which would be responsive to this situation.

1.
Your students are constantly interrupting one another in their discussions. That in itself poses no major problem, but four or five of your students have ceased to participate in the discussion. When you spoke with them, they explained their reluctance to talk because they felt that their comments were not appreciated by the group.

You could have approached this problem in many different ways. The first way might have been to operate with the total group and work out procedures to help the group become more accepting of other people's comments. An objective such as the following might have conveyed the process you had in mind.

> In group discussions, participants will let the speaker complete his or her comment before interrupting.

This objective can be measured by observational techniques. The students may not be told they are being observed by the teacher, but the teacher may compare the number of interruptions at the beginning of the course with the number of interruptions in a discussion at the end of the year. Naturally, measures of this type have nothing to do with grading of students, although after the observations are over, the students may be informed of what happened. (Obviously you would not want to tell students before the observations period because you want to be sure genuine rather than phoney responses are being displayed.)

Another way to approach the problem is to concentrate on the four individuals who feel that their comments were not sufficiently important. You might wish to formulate an objective which was directed to the needs of these students. However, such a procedure is less useful. It will be unlikely that a teacher can transform a given student's tendency to be reticent, especially under vigorous discussion situations. For illustration, an objective such as the following might have been developed.

> Each student will be able to formulate and express his or her views so that the group attends to what he or she is saying.

This objective, of course, does not mean that everyone adopts an identical style, that is, that everyone in the class will employ rapier wit and dazzling repartée. But the teacher could help each student to say what he wants to say, in his own way.

Consider this second situation. See if you can formulate a *process* objective which relates to the problem presented. Answer by Number 2 on your answer sheet.

2.

Imagine that you find yourself with a class of students who are working on a research project. The students have divided themselves into groups, not on the basis of ability, but according to interest expressed for various topics. You discover that one person, usually an achieving girl, is doing all the project work for each group. Try to formulate a process objective to solve the problem (unless you believe in exploiting women, in which case your turn will come).

You might also formulate the objective as follows:

> Group members will keep personal logs of committee meetings and write evaluative comments regarding the relative contribution of each group member.

On the other hand, you could formulate the problem much more specifically, and rather than focusing on overall group participation as the goal to be measured, you might direct your concern to the particular members of the group who are

doing the work. For instance, if the achieving girls are contributing because they dominate the activity and will not delegate authority, any objective which you formulate should include heightening their awareness of their activities. Such an objective can be measured, of course, on a self-report measure in which students are asked to describe their role in the group. On the other hand, the girls may have been working hard because no one else will participate. While the objective may be measured the same way, you should be able to see that very different actions are implied by the teacher.

Objectives such as the ones previously noted are not commonly perceived as proper subject matter for behavioral or operational objectives. But they meet the two criteria previously outlined: they are important and they can be measured.

If you are teaching now or expect to be doing so soon in a school where the use of objectives is indicated, you can strongly affect the tenor of activity if you insist that objectives be included which measure the process of learning the students' attitudes and feelings about it. The purpose of such objectives is clearly not to assist in the budgeting of funds. (Apparently, only reading test scores have any effect there.) But systematically gathering such information and talking it over with teacher colleagues can help you make your classroom a more exciting and pleasant place to be, in addition to whatever other objectives you are presently teaching.

The second major way to "humanize" the use of instructional objectives in your particular setting requires the serious involvement of the students in the selection and development of the instructional goals which they feel they need to learn. This does not mean asking, "What do you want to do today?" but rather is a specific procedure which can demonstrate to students that they can substantially contribute to the nature of the instructional offering and that their contribution is not viewed casually or solicited as a ploy to "buy them off." Suppose you are the teacher in an English class and do not have complete freedom to develop your own curriculum. You are limited by your own time commitments, the available textbooks, certain school or departmental requirements. You might feel that you have very little freedom in determining your instructional goals, but you surely have great latitude in deciding exactly what it is that the students can learn.

Most formulation of instructional goals is conducted by teachers, working singly or in groups. The individual teacher who develops a set of objectives may do so by going into a deep trance while staring at the required text. Curriculum committees which prepare objectives, while motivated by positive values, may ultimately select objectives because the most vocal participant argues strongly for a particular set. Humanizing this process is easy and extremely rewarding. You merely must involve students in the decision-making activity. And there are ways for securing student involvement. A completely open situation is likely to be an unsuccessful way to get useful output from the students. A recommended procedure has been called by the technical sounding phrase, "needs-assessment." The teacher explains to the students that they are going to help determine what they are going to be learning during the school year. A list of areas of interest to the class and to the teacher is jointly prepared. Students thus help the teacher operationalize the general goal areas. To do this, the teacher must simply ask "What would you be doing if you were successful in this area?"—the time-honored heuristic for generating instructional objectives. The student and teacher cooperatively develop a set of tentative instructional objectives. Thus, the first two steps of student-based needs-assessment are:

1. Teacher explains *purpose* of the needs-assessment.
2. Students and teacher cooperatively develop set of objectives.

The second step may be impractical for very young learners. In such case, the teacher develops the tentative list of objectives alone and brings them into class. Places for the students to add to the list should be provided.

The third step in this process is to develop priorities among the objectives. Try to think of some ways in which priorities for instructional objectives could be determined. Answer by Number 3 on your answer sheet.

You might have included a number of procedures. First, objectives which interest students can be determined. Second, students' needs in terms of unmastered objectives can be evaluated. Third, students' and teacher's estimate of the importance of various objectives can be measured. More specifically, how can objectives be ordered in priority form? To find answers to questions of interest, need, and importance of instructional goals, solid information is required. The teacher working with the class can easily develop appropriate questionnaires to find out which objectives have most student interest and which are rated as most important. These questionnaires are then given to all the students in the class and results publicly tabulated. If the students become very much involved in the process of curriculum building, they may wish to investigate other sources for their data. For instance, they may wish to give their questionnaire to students in upper grades to determine if older and wiser cohorts have the same values. They may also wish to involve their parents or other members of the community or additional members of the teaching staff. Regardless of the groups to whom the questionnaire is administered, the critical point is that the students themselves have been participating in an educational process and have made the significant choices on their own.

To review, so far the steps in humanizing the process of developing objectives have been sketched something like this:

1. Teacher explains purpose of the needs assessment.
2. Students and teacher cooperatively develop set of objectives.
3. Develop priorities among objectives by preparing a questionnaire which measures interest and importance of objectives.

A further note on the development of the questionnaire is in order. No elaborate psychometric procedure is implied here. Simple items phrased like the following are well within the competence of all teachers and most students.

Which objectives interest you? Rate them 1–5 by circling the number next to each objective.
1. To write research papers on population problems

no interest				very interested
1	2	3	4	5

A second critical step in the development of priorities for instructional objectives is to determine what the students' present performance levels are. In cases where exotic objectives are being developed, such pretesting isn't necessary, for it is unlikely that the students have any measurable competence in the area.

However, for many objectives, the students might be given short tests to determine how much they know at the present time. Objectives where students' performance is very low would then be especially noted in the establishment of priorities. The final step is a joint judgment by students and teacher.

3. Develop priorities among objectives by
    (A) Preparing and administering questionnaire on interest and importance.
    (B) Pretesting students to find out present performance.
    (C) Making a judgment based on information.

Teachers may begin to get worried regarding the issue of control and responsibility when objectives are generated by heavily involving students in every significant decision. Yet, some abrogation of power and authority is necessary if the activity is to be genuine. In situations where the teacher is heavily constrained by school organization, the students should be involved in the selection of goals in as many areas as possible. The limitations of the teachers' situation should be explained to them if they are old enough to understand. And the explanation should be tactful.

See if you can list the steps in involving students in the development and selection of objectives. There are three main points and three sub-steps for the last point. Answer by Number 4 on your answer sheet.

4.
1. _____
2. _____
3. _____
   (A) _____
   (B) _____
   (C) _____

1. Teacher explains purpose of needs assessment.
2. Students and teachers cooperatively develop sets of objectives.
3. Students and teachers develop priorities among objectives by
   (A) Preparing questionnaire on interest.
   (B) Pretesting students on performance.
   (C) Making judgments about information.

Naturally, the extent to which you are able to implement this procedure is limited by factors other than whether you have a school situation which permits you a great deal of freedom. The nature of your student group is also important. More freedom can be given to older students in general; but young children, even those at the first-grade level, can profit greatly from a modified version of the procedure. Whatever the level you teach, be prepared for some new and exciting objectives. Be prepared as well for a great deal of acceptance by your students.

So far we have sketched two ways to humanize the use of educational objectives in the classroom. The first recommendation required that the objectives include process goals which foster respect for the individual. The second recommendation described the involvement of the students in the development of instructional objectives. The determination of goals would be a joint responsibility of student and teacher.

1. Use objectives that encourage respect for the individual.
2. Involve students in the determination of their own goals.

The third recommendation regarding the use of instructional objectives centers on procedures for *implementation* rather than development. The emphasis here is primarily on instruction. Among the flagrant misunderstandings regarding the use and intent of objectives is the notion that students must be homogenized by their encounter with objectives. For instance, because a set of objectives has been developed, critics assume that all students will receive identical instruction. Further, that instruction is likely to be structured, heavily didactic, and dependent upon lecture and exercises as the probable mode of teaching. Such gloomy and mechanistic descriptions of course can characterize objectives-based instruction, but probably with the same incidence as instruction perpetrated without objectives. Poor teaching is probably equally distributed across ideologies. However, objectives can provide a useful tool to assist in making the instructional part of the school experience more satisfying for the students.

One procedure for "humanizing" the use of educational objectives was hinted at in an early example. Objectives may be differentiated for students, so that every student will have a different array of objectives which he or she is seeking to attain. In the earlier example, the objective dealing with self-confidence to participate in a spirited classroom discussion was suitable for only the four or five students who kept silent. Suitability of objectives for students can be determined by using the information gained during the needs-assessment procedure. The teacher and students can review performance, interest, and importance ratings of given objectives and develop an individualized program for a given student.

Although differentiation by objective is a great way to begin to deal with the reality of student variety in ability, interests and values, it should be clear that certain objectives may be shared by the entire group. For instance, objectives in fields such as reading or composition may be important enough that all students should be able to demonstrate a minimal competence with them.

Implementation
1. Different objectives for different students

Another procedure you can use to help make the use of objectives more satisfying to the individual is to inform the student of the exact goals he should attain. If objectives are cooperatively developed, this problem is partly solved. Yet, many times teachers prepare sets of objectives and keep them hidden from the students. Clearly identifying the objectives and, hopefully, the procedures by which the objectives will be evaluated, can substantially improve the instructional environment. Students are not used to being "let in on" the goals of instruction. If told the objectives, they can direct their attention to the areas of concern rather than waste time trying to outguess the teacher.

Let's review some of the major points in this program. The first recommendation involved the preparation of objectives which were process-oriented and directed to provide help for the learner's personal and social development rather than his subject matter acquisition. Write such an objective by Number 5 on your answer sheet.

If you are reading this program in a group situation, you might wish to exchange papers with a classmate and ask for his evaluation of your objective. Otherwise, inspect it to see whether social progress or personal development is its substance. Check it also to determine if it is operationally stated, that is, phrased so that it can be observed.

The second recommendation centered upon involving students as colleagues in the development of objectives. A detailed needs-assessment procedure was outlined. See if you can reproduce its essential elements by Number 6 on your answer sheet.

6.
Needs Assessment
1. _____
2. _____
3. _____
  (A) _____
  (B) _____
  (C) _____

1. Teacher explains purpose of needs assessment.
2. Students and teachers cooperatively develop sets of objectives.
3. Students and teachers develop priorities among objectives by
  (A) Preparing questionnaire on interest.
  (B) Pretesting students on performance.
  (C) Making judgments about information.

Last of all, list two particular ways of implementing objectives so that more satisfying learning environments are developed. Answer by Number 7 on your answer sheet.

7.

Implementation

1.

2.

---

1. Different objectives for different students.
2. Inform students of the objectives.

It is possible that this entire presentation struck you as not very humanistic itself. Some responses were asked of you, but because of the relative brevity of the program it was difficult to deal with the range of concerns and objections you might have to instructional objectives. As a final attempt, consider a singularly important benefit to the use of instructional objectives. The explication of objectives provides an

"YOUR OBJECTIVE IF YOU DECIDE TO ACCEPT IS TO LEARN TO......"

PHONE

element of choice to the student. He or she is not to be deluded by the teacher. If he or she wishes to attend and participate in the instruction, it is because of a strong understanding of the outcome. This situation is quite apart from the more usual case, in which a teacher can characterize instruction in seductive language such as—

> You are going to become a true interpreter of classical music.

when the measures the teacher uses and the activities planned consist of memorizing isolated fact—

> Who wrote Beethoven's Ninth Symphony? Explain why in 25 words or less.

Remember, the program advocates specific ways to humanize the use of objectives.

> 1. The use of objectives that encourage respect for the individual.
> 2. Student involvement in choosing objectives.
> 3. Implementation of objectives.

We hope the presentation suggested to you some alternative possibilities for the use of objectives. You can very likely think of more. Try some.

Deciding on Defensible Goals via Educational Needs Assessment

Objectives

This program outlines a specific procedure which educators may employ to select their educational goals more judiciously. The strategy examined in the program is usually referred to as an *educational needs assessment* and has been used with increasing frequency during recent years at local and state levels. Partially to permit the assessment of this general aim, the following measurable objective can be employed for the program.

> After completing the program the learner, using a real or ficticious educational situation, will be able to prepare a written plan for an educational needs assessment procedure which is judged superior to a comparable plan prepared prior to the program.

Recent attention given to the field of instructional psychology augers well for new emphasis on providing teachers with the technical skills they need to accomplish worthwhile educational objectives. But even as we applaud the prospect of more instructionally proficient teachers, we can contemplate the serious problem which such a situation produces. If teachers become more skilled at achieving changes in learners, what kinds of changes should they pursue? Putting it another way, what kinds of goals should our teachers be trying to accomplish? An increase in a teacher's instructional skill makes it more imperative that he or she pursue truly defensible goals.

This program will describe a step-by-step procedure for deciding on defensible educational goals through a technique referred to as *educational needs assessment*. This procedure can be used at any level of education where goals must be determined: the individual teacher's classroom, the local school district, or the statewide school system. In general, the larger the educational system involved, the more elaborate the procedure.

Throughout the program you will be asked to assume the roles of different people—such as parents, community leaders, or school curriculum workers—and to make a decision or supply some information consistent with your assumed role. Thus, by seeing the kinds of data necessary to make such a needs assessment system function, you should be better able to anticipate some of the procedural difficulties which are associated with such goal determination schemes. At the close of the program you should be able to design an educational needs assessment strategy which, although it may be at variance with some of the specific suggestions you are about to encounter, should provide you with a practical method of deciding on defensible educational goals.

To begin, let's examine the key element of an educational needs assessment strategy, that is, an *educational need.* This phrase, often used by educators, holds a number of interpretations.

Assume that you are a *school curriculum specialist* who has just been asked by a parent to define the phrase *educational need.* How would you do it? In a few words on the response sheet beside Number 1, briefly define an educational need.

You probably responded that an educational need represents some sort of deficiency which can hopefully be alleviated through education. Here is a somewhat more technical, though generally accepted, conception of an educational need:

A desired learner outcome	–	Learner's current status	=	An educational need

By first identifying what kinds of learner behavior we desire, then contrasting the learner's current behavior with what we desire, we can identify the gap between what we want and what we have. Generally, this difference is referred to as an educational need. Educators are concerned with such needs because curricular goals can be established by identifying those needs most in need of amelioration. If a school district is rationally trying to decide on a set of goals around which to organize its educational efforts, it must isolate the most significant educational needs in the district's children, then set educational goals which are designed to correct such deficiencies.

Notice that the type of educational need we have been discussing is *exclusively* based on some desired change we are attempting to bring about in our learners, for example, in their intellectual skills or attitudinal predispositions. This is consistent with the general point of view that it is the mission of the school to promote worthwhile modifications in learners. A few people mistakenly try to define educational needs in terms of the physical or personnel needs of a school system, for example, textbooks, school buses, or counselors. But our conception of educational need definitely focuses on the learner, not the instructional vehicles we assume will help learners. Let's examine four steps designed to isolate learner needs.

Step One: Identify educational preferences

The first step in most educational needs assessment schemes is to identify the sorts of behavior we prefer our learners to possess. If we had our way with school age children, what would we like the kids to be like when they were finished with school? We might want to focus on particular intermediate points during a child's educational life, rather than waiting until it is completely over (a third-grade teacher is probably most concerned with what her children will be like at the end of third grade, not when they get out of college).

But the prime difficulty in previous efforts by curriculum workers was that the preferences were not isolated in a reliable or usable form. For one thing, if preferences were gathered, they were usually stated in terms, such as "love of country," which were too broad to be of much guidance. Secondly, educational preferences were often gathered exclusively from prestigious, blue ribbon commissions which failed to include representatives of the very groups most concerned with education, that is, the parents, the teachers, and the children themselves.

Here are several alternative tactics which might be employed to get a reasonable fix on what we want learners to be like as a consequence of their education.

One technique employs open-ended questionnaires or loosely structured interviews with various groups whose views regarding the school system are important. For instance, a local school district interviews a sample of (1) parents, (2) children, (3) teachers, and (4) nonparent citizens, asking them to: "Describe the behaviors you would like children to exhibit at the end of twelve years of public school." Imagine, for a moment, that you are a fifty-year-old *businessman* with no children. How would you respond to such a question? Try to describe one behavior you would like children to display at the close of a twelve-year public school education. Write the essence of your answer next to Number 2 on the response sheet.

If your response was typical, it was stated in pretty general terms. And such general statements are particularly difficult and troublesome to coalesce meaningfully when they have been supplied by a number of different people, particularly when the people represent quite disparate groups. Usually someone is faced with the onerous task of recording a morass of divergent preferences, stated at all levels of generality. If the person or persons conducting such an analysis can accomplish it insightfully and objectively, then the resulting statements regarding preferences will be useful.

A second approach to securing preferences developed recently as a consequence of several objectives-bank agencies such as the Instructional Objectives Exchange* assembling large collections of measurable instructional objectives, that is, objectives stated in terms of learner postinstructional behavior. Sometimes referred to as behavioral objectives or performance objectives, these goal statements communicate far less ambiguously what it is intended that the learner be able to do after instruction and, therefcre, they provide the possibility of reducing the confusion when diverse groups express educational preferences.

Suppose a number of objectives were selected from one or more of the measurable objectives collections, then were given to different groups who would rate them according to their perceived appropriateness for the schools. Imagine for a

*Box 24095, Los Angeles, California 90024

moment that you, a *parent* of a sixth-grade child, are asked to rate the following objective according to your estimate of whether it reflects a type of behavior you would like your sixth-grade child to attain. Rate the objective on a scale 5 (feel very strongly) to 1 (don't want it included) depending on how strongly you feel about the objective's inclusion in the curriculum. Answer by Number 3 on the response sheet. Remember you should rate the objective as though you were a parent.

3.

Having read a current events report, e.g., a newspaper article, of several hundred words length, the learner will be able to summarize its main point(s) accurately in one sentence.

It is hard to predict, of course, just how important you considered this objective. But imagine that you had ratings supplied for a number of such objectives by a variety of different groups. By averaging these ratings you could obtain a general estimate of how important each group believed each objective to be. Suppose 25 parents, 100 children, and 25 academic subject matter experts rated a group of history objectives on a five-point scale and came up with the following ratings. If you were a curriculum worker charged with the responsibility of selecting the objectives most preferred by these different groups, which of the following objectives should you select? Write the number of that objective by Number 4 on the response sheet.

4.

Average Objective Ratings
(5=important, 1=unimportant)

Objective	Parents	Students	Academicians
#1	3.8	2.4	3.9
#2	4.2	3.2	2.7

#3	3.4	4.2	4.3
#4	1.6	4.2	1.9

Assuming that the average ratings of the three groups are weighted equally, you should have selected objective number three as the most preferred. Such summary ratings can subsequently be used to secure a *ranked* set of objectives arranged according to those most preferred. It is possible, of course, to assign different weights to the contributions of various groups.

Now imagine you were a *school principal* and were going to be *bound* by the expressed preferences of the three groups presented here, that is, you were going to try to emphasize in the curriculum those objectives receiving the highest ratings and try to deemphasize those receiving the lowest ratings. Could you see yourself weighting the preferences of one of these three groups more heavily than another? If so, which group? Answer by Number 5 on the answer sheet.

Responses to this kind of a question vary considerably. Just about as many educators favor disproportionate weighting as those who favor equal weighting. Opinions vary, too, as far as which group might be given the most influence. The important point is that if dissimilar weightings are to be assigned to different groups, this difference in influence potential can be made visible and decided on the basis of open discussion.

And this brings up a point which educators have to face squarely if they are thinking of using an educational needs assessment scheme to isolate instructional goals. The more *explicit* the procedures are for deciding on educational goals, the less likelihood that personal preferences will dictate what the goals should be. Let's use the dissimilar weighting possibility as an example. As long as curriculum goals are decided as they are at present, in a confusing maze of more or less rational decision making, no one can really know whose influence is paramount. Hence, if a curriculum worker wants parents to be more influential, he can emphasize those goals he thinks they will like without anyone else knowing. A *visible* system for goal determination makes such sub rosa decisions less likely. To secure meaningful participation of various groups in the goal decision process, certain curriculum prerogatives will have to be given up.

But while we are still considering ways of identifying preferences, we should examine some alternatives. Individuals can also make matched pair comparisons between all possible paired combinations of objectives. To illustrate, imagine now that you are a first year *high school student* and have been asked to choose which of the following two objectives you would most like to see included in your own curriculum. Choose either objective A or B, then circle the appropriate letter on the response sheet next to Number 6.

6.
A. Be able to prove geometric theorems.
B. Be able to calculate square foot areas of any geometric shape given sufficient dimension measurements.

When these two objectives were given to a small sample of high school students, most opted for objective B. But using a matched pair comparison technique which, incidentally, is explained in most educational measurement textbooks, objective B would also be paired with all other objectives; thus, by analyzing the results of all paired comparisons a precise overall ranking could be obtained for the entire set of objectives.

But if there are many objectives involved, as you have probably guessed, the total number of required comparisons rises dramatically. Therefore, an important requirement in any large scale needs assessment operation is that *person and item sampling techniques be employed.* Most educators are familiar with person sampling whereby responses from small numbers of individuals are used to reflect those of an entire group. Item sampling developed more recently. Put simply, item sampling permits different individuals to rate, or rank, or make paired comparisons for less than the total number of objectives to be considered. For example, if we had 100 objectives to be rated by 200 parents, we might give each of four groups of 50 parents 25 objectives to rate, or give each 20 parents only 10 different objectives to rate. We could still secure a reasonably reliable estimate of the preferences of the group, yet save much time in securing the data.

Our review of the several alternatives to identifying preferences points up an obvious common dimension. Different groups are being consulted and their preferences can vary

considerably. Perhaps they will be asked to rate objectives drawn from objectives banks; perhaps they will be asked to rank different types of descriptions of learner behavior. Certainly there can be all sorts of procedural variations in the way a needs assessor secures preferences, but by consulting those clienteles concerned with the education of the learners involved, a more defensible set of preferences can surely be secured.

For example, imagine you are a *teacher* in an economically disadvantaged inner city elementary school who has been asked to rank the importance of a set of fifteen hoped-for learner behaviors. Do you think your rankings will look very much like those you would supply if you were teaching in an affluent suburban area? Answer Yes or No next to Number 7 on answer sheet.

Probably you answered no, for while we have undoubtedly many common expectations for our children irrespective of where they go to school, we also have some pretty ideosyncratic instructional requirements which arise from a given educational setting. The more particularized we can make our needs assessment, the better.

Thus, we can graphically depict the scheme for securing educational preferences as follows, whereby various concerned clienteles have an opportunity to offer input to those preferences which will ultimately guide us.

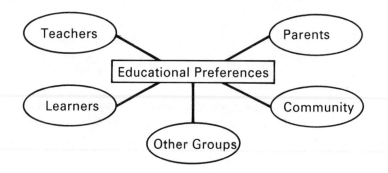

Note that beyond the more customary selections of teachers, parents, and children, other groups can be consulted. In some successful educational needs assessments a group of *futurists* is specially formed to rank educational objectives according to their suitability for a society of the 1980s or 1990s. Some educators wish to weight such preferences even heavier than those of groups which are enamoured of the status quo.

But surely, after these numerous examples, you have an idea of how educational preferences can be secured for a needs assessment. We can readily imagine a teacher's securing goal preferences from her students, the parents of her students, and a group of her colleagues—just to get a better fix on their preferences for her own instructional situation. Given some time, you will probably be able to think of even better ways of accomplishing this first step in a needs assessment. Step one should result in a ranked list of instructional objectives, somewhat larger in number than the final number expected to be selected at the close of the needs assessment. Let's turn now to the second operation.

Step Two: Establish mastery proportions

Once we have a reasonable number of statements describing the kinds of learner behavior which are most preferred (if possible arranged in rank order) the next task is to decide what proportion of learners we really want to possess that behavior. For instance, some behaviors should probably be achieved by almost all learners, while others need be achieved by only a few. Step two in our needs assessment scheme involves establishing the proportions of learners whom we wish to master those most preferred behaviors identified in step one. We do this as a second step to avoid the necessity of establishing mastery proportions for many behaviors which will not even end up among our most preferred.

Now imagine you are a university *professor,* a member of a representative group specially constituted to supply mastery proportions for twenty-five highly ranked goal statements. What proportion of learners leaving high school do you think ought to be able to master the following two behaviors? Supply the mastery percentage for each beside Number 8 on the answer sheet.

8.

A. Be able to write an original paragraph of 50 or more words which contains no grammatical errors.

B. Be able to calculate the correct change due a purchaser in a variety of routine business transactions, e.g., buying groceries.

Of course it's difficult to judge what your recommended mastery percentages were in each case, but probably the percentage for objective B was closer to 100 than that for objective A. It is reasonable that we would want to produce very few citizens who could not display the behavior called for in objective B. The behavior in objective A is probably somewhat less critical.

Thus, using some type of group judgment, either calling on a smaller number of people or essentially repeating the process described earlier in step one, the second phase of our needs assessment scheme should yield some sort of consensus-derived estimates of what percentages of our learners we wish to master the highest ranked objectives. The product of step two would look something like this:

Rank of objective	Desired mastery percentages
#1	84%
#2	71%
#3	96%
#4	92%
#5	65%
etc.	etc.

Step Three: Identify current learner status

As we turn to step three, we find out what the learners' current behavior is like. For each of the high ranked objectives still under consideration, measures must be employed to assess the current proportion of learners who can display mastery of the objective. Incidentally, mastery is used in a somewhat loose sense here, for if the objective is attitudinal in nature, it doesn't sound quite right to say the student has "mastered" the objective. What we really want to know is the proportion of learners in the target population who do (or can) display the desired behavior.

In many instances you will have to construct appropriate measuring devices to accomplish step three satisfactorily.

(You may have already realized why most existing commercial tests are inappropriate.) Beside Number 9 on the answer sheet indicate why most available standardized tests are unsuitable for this type of assessment.

Most available standardized tests are unsuitable because they are *norm-referenced,* that is, they are designed to permit measurements which will allow contrasts between individuals, not to permit precise judgment about how learners behave with respect to specific objectives. Fortunately, several of the previously mentioned objectives-bank agencies already make available criterion-referenced tests which can be used to measure their objectives. Some items can also be drawn from existing tests—even standardized tests—and adapted. The crucial thing is to employ measuring procedures which are totally congruent with the objectives under consideration. An objective which calls for learner behavior *X* and a test which measures *Y* just won't do.

The measures are then administered to a large enough sample of learners to yield a reliable estimate of what the total group's current status is. Results of these measurement operations are then displayed next to the desired mastery proportions already established as a result of step two. Thus, we can readily see the proportion of learners we want to have attained each objective and the proportion of learners who actually have. A display such as the following, then, is the product of step three in our needs assessment system.

Rank of objective	Desired mastery percentages	Actual mastery percentages
#1	84%	87%
#2	71%	41%
#3	96%	56%
#4	92%	89%
#5	65%	21%
etc.	etc.	etc.

The fourth and final step in this scheme involves a decision regarding which goals should be pursued based on an analysis of such data as that presented here.

> *Step Four:* Select goals by contrasting desired status with current learner status

Assume an imaginary role and make believe you are the *director of a statewide needs assessment* deciding which of these objectives should be recommended for emphasis throughout the state's educational system. Circle the numbers of any objectives you would choose beside Number 10 on the response sheet.

10.

Rank of objective	Desired mastery percentages	Actual mastery percentages
#1	84%	87%
#2	71%	41%
#3	96%	56%
#4	92%	89%
#5	65%	21%
etc.	etc.	etc.

You probably selected objectives two, three, and five, since those are the goals for which the disparity between preference and reality is the greatest. On the other two objectives, learner attainments more closely approximate our desires, so there is less need for educational amelioration.

Of course, the degree of sophistication you exercise in this final phase of the needs assessment operation should depend on the magnitude of the operation at hand. There are some really tricky problems involved here, for do we emphasize the *rank* of the objective or the *gap* between desired and actual mastery percentages? If conducted in a large school system or at a statewide level, our needs assessment could employ all sorts of choice-sharpening refinements at this point. A teacher or a group of teachers conducting their own needs assessments can follow less complex decision rules.

In review, then, we have examined some, but not all, of the nuances associated with a systematic effort to decide on educational goals through the use of educational needs assessment strategy. The following four steps were considered in some detail:

Step One: Identify educational preferences
Step Two: Establish mastery proportions
Step Three: Identify current learner status
Step Four: Select goals by contrasting desired status with current learner status

Closing your eyes for a moment, see if you can recall these four operations.

Whether employed in one class of eighteen children or in an entire state with thousands of learners, methods comparable to those described here should aid educators in selecting goals which are truly defensible. Hopefully, if asked to design

a needs assessment procedure for your own educational situation you could do so more satisfactorily. Remember, the better educators become at instructing people, the more crucial it is that they select the proper goals.

Identifying Affective Objectives

Objectives

Although the current state of knowledge regarding how affective objectives can be assessed dissatisfies educational measurement specialists, there is clearly a need for some guidance for those concerned with this important area of measurement. This program outlines a strategy which has proved useful to those involved in the specification of affective objectives.

Specifically, after the conclusion of the program the learner will be able to:

1. Describe the strategy recommended in the program for identifying measurable affective objectives.
2. When presented with a previously unencountered nonbehavioral objective in the affective domain, generate a greater number of measurable affective objectives than he was able to before completing the program.

During the last several years educators have become increasingly attentive to the form in which their instructional objectives should be described. They have pervasively pushed toward more precision in the manner in which educational goals should be stated. Vague, general objectives have been replaced, at least at the instructional level, with explicit descriptions of the learner behaviors to be promoted. Teachers are being urged to describe their instructional intentions exclusively in terms of *measurable* learner behaviors, for by observing whether such behaviors are present after instruction the teacher can judge if his instructional sequence was successful. Indeed, operationally stated objectives have been nationally advocated in this country and, unlike certain other educational movements, promise to be with us for some time to come. The advocacy of behaviorally stated objectives is not analogous to the advocacy of "Method A" or "Method B." Rather, it represents a quest for clarity of intention. Such clarity is the cornerstone of rational decision making in any intellectual arena—and education is surely one of the most important of these.

A corollary concern to the form of objectives is the substance of these goals. Are our increasingly efficient instructional systems directed toward the proper ends?

We now hear with increasing frequency phrases like "high cognitive," "affective," and "low cognitive" tossed about at meetings of teachers and curriculum planners. These phrases are based on the classification efforts of Professor Benjamin Bloom, David Krathwohl, and their associates. Many educators have found that the constructs devised by these individuals in connection with the *Taxonomies of Educational Objectives* are useful in considering alternative instructional objectives. This program will be devoted to one aspect of this question, namely, the identification of *affective* instructional objectives.

Assuming that you are somewhat familiar with this three-domain scheme used to classify objectives as either cognitive, affective, or psychomotor, let's try a practice exercise for review. Next to Number 1 on your answer sheet indicate whether the following objectives are primarily cognitive (C), affective (A), or psychomotor (P).

1.
A. Learner is able to multiply correctly any pair of three-digit numbers.
B. Student can kick soccer ball fifty yards.
C. Learner exclusively selects mysteries during free reading periods.

You should have indicated that A was primarily a cognitive behavior, B a psychomotor behavior, and C an affective behavior. Let's briefly review the boundaries of these three behavior domains. The *cognitive* domain includes all objectives which deal with the intellectual behaviors of the learner. In the previous exercise, the learner who was able to multiply correctly was engaging in what was primarily an intellectual, or "mental," behavior.

The *psychomotor* domain covers all those objectives in which the learner is engaged in some physical, kinesthetic behavior. Playing the piano or using an adding machine with competence requires manual dexterity and muscle control. These are the sorts of behaviors included in the psychomotor domain. In the previous exercise, the ability to kick a soccer ball fifty yards is an instance of a psychomotor skill.

The *affective* domain is concerned with the attitudes, feelings, interests, and values of the learner. Although it may be technically impossible to assert that this is noncognitive (for there is surely admixture of cognition in most learner interest and values), this domain should be restricted to such noncognitive outcomes as the way a student *feels* (not *thinks*) about a given phenomenon. In the previous exercise a preference for mysteries would be properly classified in the affective domain for it reflects the learner's values regarding reading matter.

Next to Number 2 on the answer sheet classify each of these general educational objectives as cognitive (C), affective (A), or psychomotor (P).

2.
The learner will:
A. Learn to enjoy poetry.
B. Develop quantitative competence.
C. Become a good citizen.
D. Be able to use a typewriter.
E. Be able to write lucid prose.

Objectives B and E were cognitive. Objectives A and C were affective. Objective D was psychomotor.

The cognitive and psychomotor domains are concerned with the question: What *can* the learner do? The affective domain, on the other hand, is concerned with the question: What *will* the learner do? Both questions, of course, are of concern to educators. But although we have made some progress in developing instructional objectives in the cognitive and psychomotor domains, our sophistication regarding the identification of affective goals is minimal; only recently have educators and other behavioral scientists attacked questions of measurement in the affective domain with any kind of concerted effort. It will probably be several years before we have a systematic collection of theory and empirical studies regarding the affective domain. But in the meantime we still must make educational decisions. More specifically, we still must decide whether we wish to achieve affective instructional objectives and, if so, which affective objectives we will seek. This program will outline a relatively simple strategy which has proved useful to those who wish to generate affective objectives.

A strategy for generating affective objectives

Let's consider the task. We usually start with a general, imprecise statement such as, "We want our learners to be interested in current affairs." If you had to classify such a broad goal, you would undoubtedly place it in the affective domain. But an affective objective, like any useful objective, must be stated in such a way that we can tell, after instruction, whether we have achieved it. In other words, it must be measurable. The difficult task is to move from a general statement of intent such as "interest in current affairs" to a description of one or more *observable* learner behaviors which reflect such an interest. Here is one scheme to identify measurable indicators of affect.

First, clearly identify for yourself the general affective dimension you are dealing with, for example, an attitude toward

some stimulus, and then imagine a learner who fully possesses that affective attribute. If you are concerned with promoting enjoyment of music, then imagine someone who is
literally consumed by his enjoyment of music. So great is his
enjoyment of music that he could be aptly characterized as a
music lover. This imaginary human can be designated as our
"attribute possessor" for such a hypothetical individual surely
has the affective attribute we are considering.

Attribute
possessor
Step One

The next step is once more to imagine someone, but this time
it must be a person who either does not possess the affective
attribute or is negative about it. This hypothetical individual
becomes our "attribute nonpossessor." In the case of interest
in music, we could imagine someone who is totally indifferent to or actually dislikes music. Obviously, our two hypothetical individuals will be at completely different ends of a
continuum describing the affective dimension in which we
are interested.

Attribute   Attribute
possessor   nonpossessor
Step One   *Step Two*

The next step is the most difficult and yet the most interesting in this strategy. You must now identify observable situations in which these two hypothetical individuals would
behave differently. These situations can be either those that
would occur naturally in the lives of the intended learners, or
those that you might contrive deliberately for purposes of
evaluation.

Attribute   Attribute
possessor   nonpossessor
Step One   *Step Two*
Difference-producing
situations
Step Three

In describing such situations you must be attentive to all contributing conditions which might reduce the tendency of

the attribute possessor to behave differently than the nonpossessor. For instance, suppose you are concerned with "interest in poetry" and, as part of step three, you identify the following behavior.

> English teacher will ask his students to raise their hands if they like poetry. He believes that only those who like poetry will raise their hands.

Do you think there will be a reliable difference in the responses of attribute possessors and nonpossessors? Answer next to Number 3 on your answer sheet.

The better answer here would be No. Some nonpossessors, that is, those who don't like poetry, might answer in a way which they think will be pleasing to the teacher, and therefore would raise their hands, thus behaving in the same way as those who do like poetry. This illustrates an important rule to be followed in identifying difference-producing situations.

Eliminate all cues which will aid the learner in knowing how he "should" behave.

In devising measures of affect we are anxious to find out what the learner will do when he is under no external pressure to behave in a particular way. Thus, we must reduce all cues which will influence spontaneous behavior. Answer the following problem next to Number 4.

4.
If you, a teacher, wanted to get responses to an attitudinal questionnaire, should you ask your students to turn them in signed or unsigned?
A.   Signed
B.   Unsigned

Clearly, unsigned questionnaires are preferable.

If you are working with a class of students you have come to know fairly well, should you have them write comments on unsigned questionnaires? Answer next to Number 5.

Because many pupils believe, and properly so, that the teacher can recognize handwriting, they might be reluctant to be candid—throughout the questionnaire—if they thought they could be identified. Hence, the teacher should use anonymous questionnaires which require only check marks—and still treat student responses with more than one grain of salt.

These comments regarding questionnaires illustrate the general rule that behavior-influencing cues should be eliminated when assessing behavior designed to measure affective objectives. It is perfectly reasonable, however, to consider the use of anonymous self-report devices, including questionnaires and attitude inventories, as means by which to discriminate between hypothetical attribute possessors and nonpossessors.

Attribute possessors *Step One*		Attribute nonpossessors *Step Two*
	Difference-producing situations *Step Three*	

In order to see the real differences between our two imaginary human beings, we might camouflage the purpose of a questionnaire by first diverting the learners' attention through some other kinds of questions and "submerging" the key question (or questions) later in the questionnaire.

But there are other kinds of situations in which we might unearth differences between those who do and don't possess a particular affective attribute. Returning to the previous example of promoting a student's interest in current affairs, can we identify any difference-producing situations? A teacher could set up a difference-producing situation in which pupils had an option to read literature which pertained to current affairs as opposed to other categories, as long as the students were not aware that their reading selections were being observed. Those who were interested in current affairs might choose *Newsweek,* while those who were interested in different kinds of affairs might choose racy paperbacks. The teacher would set up such a situation so that behavior-influencing cues were at a minimum—for example, by having a substitute teacher provide the free-reading opportunity while the

fulltime teacher surreptitiously observes the nature of pupils' volitional reading selections.

Another difference-producing situation might be the way students would respond to a series of club-joining opportunities, some clubs being more closely related to an interest in current affairs than others. With some affective outcomes, of course, it is far more difficult to identify such situations than with others. But the important thing is to generate a variety of situations which seem likely to produce differences between those who do and do not possess a given affective quality.

The final step in identifying affective objectives is to weight the alternative situations located in step three so that those can be selected which are both most likely to produce differences and also relatively easy to implement.

Attribute	Attribute
possessor	nonpossessors
Step One	*Step Two*

Difference-producing
situations
Step Three

Select
objectives
Step Four

To be useful, an affective objective must also be reasonable to measure. Some exotic difference-producing situations are completely impractical to measure. The individual deciding on the objectives may wish to call in a colleague for consultation at any point in this four step process, but outside counsel is most helpful at this final stage when the objectives are actually being selected from those observable behaviors generated in step three. Which learner responses really seem to reflect the affective component under consideration? Often another's insights regarding the validity of these learner responses will be useful.

Let's review for a moment. A four step strategy has been described for identifying affective objectives. Study this scheme for a moment for you will be asked to reproduce it.

1. Imagine an individual who possesses the affective attribute.
2. Imagine an individual who does not possess the affective attribute.
3. Generate situations in which the two hypothetical individuals will behave differently.
4. Select objectives from such situations.

Now, on the answer sheet next to Number 6 write out, in your own words, the four steps to be followed in this strategy.

6.
1. _____
2. _____
3. _____
4. _____

These were the four steps:

1. Imagine an individual who possesses the affective attribute.

2. Imagine an individual who does not possess the affective attribute.
3. Generate situations in which the two hypothetical individuals will behave differently.
4. Select objectives from such situations.

Now that you have identified the situations and learner behaviors, how do you apply such objectives? For example, suppose one of your objectives was for a greater proportion of your general science students to enroll in elective upper-division science courses than the usual school average, which has been 32 percent over the past five years. Note that in this case everyone does not have to enroll in the elective classes for the percentage to increase. However, many affective objectives will call for 100 percent attainment on the part of all students. Since an instructor usually employs affective objectives as an index of his own instructional effectiveness, not as a basis for grades, it is perfectly acceptable to sample the behavior of the total class by observing randomly selected learners drawn from the whole class. Since observing learner behavior is often time-consuming—for example, if a child's relationship to peers during recess period is to be studied—the teacher can quite legitimately sample from the class and use the behavior of only a few pupils as an estimate of the whole class.

Subject-matter
approaching tendencies

$$\text{Before instruction} \quad \leq \quad \text{After instruction}$$

Let's try to use the strategy again to identify affective objectives dealing with an important general goal, namely, developing positive attitudes toward a particular subject matter. Robert Mager describes this attribute as "subject-matter approaching tendencies" and observes that after instruction such tendencies should equal or exceed those the learner displayed when he commenced the instructional sequence. In loose language, we want the students to "like" our subject. For this example let's use a history class; we want our students to be more interested in history at the close of our class than when they start. Many history teachers have such a pious goal, but usually do little to measure their success in achieving it.

First we have to conjecture what a learner who really was interested in history would be like. What kind of person would he be? What would he like to do, not like to do? Then, imagining the converse, we conjure up a hypothetical learner who is completely indifferent to history, perhaps even negative toward it. What would he be like? Now try to identify situations, either natural or contrived, in which these two hypothetical individuals would behave differently. Here are a few possible contenders. Do you think these situations would produce observable differences in behavior?

Learner's choices of historical versus nonhistorical novels in a required unit on the novel in English class. Selection of novel is left to student.

Number of students who elect to take world history course during senior year. (Other choices are Advanced English, Economics, Physical Education, Art, and Music.)

Student responses to a "forced-choice" interest inventory returned anonymously to homeroom teacher. They must express interest in one member of subject matter pairs, some of which involve history. For example:

Directions: Choose the one member of each pair in which you are more interested.

____English vs. ____history
____science vs. ____math
____math vs. ____art
____history vs. ____science

(Note: Score computed by counting number of history choices.)

These are only a few situations in which a possessor of interest in history might differ from a nonpossessor of such inter-

est. In the space by Numbers 7 and 8 on your answer sheet
see if you can describe two more.

Now examine your suggestions. To make sure that learner
responses in the situations would accurately reflect differences between those who were and those who were not
interested in history, be certain that no cues guide the learners to how they "should" respond. If there are no such cues
and you really think that an attribute possessor would behave
differently than an attribute nonpossessor, then your answers
are acceptable.

The next step is to select your affective objective or objectives from the several alternatives now available to you.
Which learner behaviors seem most indicative of interest in

history? Which behaviors can be economically assessed with the resources at your disposal? What proportion of your class do you wish to display the hoped-for behaviors? A final affective objective might look something like this.

> At the end of the term at least 20 percent more of my pupils will check history as a potential college major on questionnaires administered by the educational counselor than those who checked history at the start of the term.

Let's try using this strategy in one final practice exercise. Suppose you were trying to improve your pupils' tolerance of the opinions of others, how would you measure such an affective goal?

Respect for the opinions of others

Following the strategy recommended in this program, identify two or three situations which would constitute a basis for measuring this affective attribute. Answer next to Number 9 on the answer sheet. Devote several minutes to this task so that you can generate some worthwhile affective objectives. It may be helpful to exchange papers to get another's opinion of your objectives. In conclusion, it is hoped the strategy recommended here for identifying affective outcomes will be of some help to you. Now try to use it in measuring a learner's respect for the opinions of others.

Defining
Content
for Objectives

Objectives

The goal of this program is to promote a more moderate position with respect to the distinction between the substance and form of an educational objective. Recent attention in the educational field regarding objectives has centered almost exclusively around the form in which instructional objectives were stated. This program deals more specifically with the content of those objectives and attempts to promote the point of view that a more useful objective will be one which covers a broad range of test items rather than one which is equivalent to a single test item. Specifically, at the conclusion of the program the learner should be able to:

1. Describe the desirable relationship an objective should have to test items.
2. Discriminate between objectives which possess content generality and those which do not.
3. Convert objectives which are equivalent to test items to those which possess content generality.

A few years ago, when curriculum workers or teachers began to analyze what comprised an educational objective, they focused their attention on the content expressed in the objective. To comprehend or to become familiar with the concept of imperialism had the same impact on the teacher—the part of the objective which was critical was the content: the concept of imperialism. And such content was derived from the various subject matter disciplines.

Current emphases on objectives have shifted the pendulum away from a concentration on the content of the goal and toward the technology of stating objectives precisely. The idea of behavioral objectives is in the ascendancy.

Behavioral objectives

Which of the following is a behavioral objective? Answer by Number 1 on your answer sheet.

1.
A.   To list the five parts of the heart.
B.   To understand the function of the circulatory system.

You should have marked A since listing is a behavioral objective and can be observed. A useful objective such as that described in choice A provides explicit guidance in evaluation, for the teacher knows what student behavior to tap in order to determine whether the instruction has been successful. Because of the objective's clarity, the teacher is also strongly guided in the selection of learning activities.

But such objectives may make many teachers uneasy. While the dividends of behavioral objectives seem obvious, there is still something peculiar about objectives such as "to list five parts of the heart." Teachers may point out that one source

of inadequacy is the level of behavior demanded by the objective. It is unfortunately true that often the operational objective and examples for the method have asked for a very low cognitive level of performance. These objectives, which might be classified as level one "knowledge" on the cognitive taxonomy, call for fairly simple operations, such as recognition or recall.

Recognition   Recall

Consider these next objectives. Which seems to demand a more complex set of operations from the learner? Answer next to Number 2 on your answer sheet.

2.

A. To identify the appropriate date with the discovery of gold in California.

B. To write an essay on the significance of discovery of gold for California.

The answer is B. The superficial content of both objectives is largely the same. The level of behavior differs.

Even with the careful insistence on objectives which call for high level cognitive processes demonstrated by relatively complex behaviors, some teachers are still skeptical about the use of operational objectives.

One reason for skepticism might be the great attention devoted to the proper operational statement of the goal and the concommitant slighting of the content part of the objective.

In the pre-behavioral days the proportion of care given to the preparation of any objective heavily emphasized content. Present emphasis by some almost excludes content considerations. For the sake of balance, and because the content of any objective is at least as important as the behavior, we propose a representation such as the following:

BEHAVIOR + CONTENT

How does one begin to devote attention to the content problem? Let's begin by examining the content portion of a number of objectives to see if there is anything common in the way they are stated.

Look at this next objective. By Number 3 copy the "content" part of the following objective on your answer sheet.

3.

To list three causes of World War I.

══

The content portion (underlined) of your objective is:

To list three causes of World War I.

The objective also contains a portion describing behavior. With this next objective copy the content portion in the space provided by Number 4.

4.

To describe, in writing, one theme of *Morte D'Arthur.*

══

The underlined section of the objective refers to the content to which the behavior is applied.

Describe, in writing, one theme of *Morte D'Arthur.*

Again, this objective also has the behavior noted which the student is to demonstrate.

Now write the content section of this objective next to Number 5 on your answer sheet.

5.

To prepare a report describing the chemical reaction of copper with sulfuric acid.

Your answer should include the section underlined as follows:

> To prepare a report describing <u>the chemical reaction of copper with sulfuric acid.</u>

"To prepare a report" refers to the behavior called for by the student. The content portions in the three preceding objectives have something in common.

> One theme of *Morte D'Arthur*
> Three causes of World War I
> The chemical reaction of copper with sulfuric acid

Each objective, while behavioral, refers to one small and specific bit of content. If a teacher were to choose the second objective, for example, he might very carefully teach students to write about a theme of *Morte D'Arthur,* but then what would he have? Students who could make the appropriate behavioral response to one small segment of literature.

Similarly students could make the correct responses to the causes of World War I and the reaction of copper with sulfuric acid, yet they would be precisely but narrowly skilled. An arch-precisionist in behaviorism might say that if theme identification is important in other works besides the one explicated in the objective, the teacher should specify all such literary works. Thus an exhaustive list might be prepared where each new theme identification would require a separate objective. Each objective would be equivalent to a test item.

Here are some objectives. Circle Yes by Number 6 if this first objective is equivalent to a test item; circle No if it is not.

6.
To be able to identify the protagonist in *Antigone*.

You should have answered Yes. The student would be responding to a specific bit of content. He would identify protagonists only in *Antigone*. Try this next example. Is this objective equivalent to a test item? Answer Yes or No by Number 7.

7.

Given a list of alternatives, to be able to select the best definition of an empty set.

You should have answered Yes, since only one particular definition was to be learned.

For this next question, determine whether the objective is equivalent to a test item. Write Yes or No next to Number 8.

8.

To translate orally the first dialog in the Spanish I book.

Again your answer should be Yes. The students would not be expected to generalize beyond the particular dialog they learned.

Specifying all objectives as test items is a time-consuming task. And when any task becomes onerous, there is less chance it will be completed. The idea of listing as separate objectives either all literature for which themes could be stated or all possible chemical reactions would make reprobates of the staunchest supporters of classroom operational objectives. Must we advocate something which teachers will have neither the time nor the inclination to do? Even cataloging content and listing objectives does not take account of future knowledge, novels-to-be, or wars to come. Explicit content does not help our students deal with new, and as yet, undiscovered content.

One rigorous method of dealing with the content problem is economical in that it does not require the extensive listing of all bits of content to which the behavior in the objective will apply. It also seems to handle the difficulty of providing a way to promote the students' ability to generalize beyond the particular particles of content they have been exposed to. Most important, the attribute of behavior in an objective is retained. The method can be called content generality. The following is an example of how such an objective might look:

> The student will be able to add two-column addition problems in which the integers range from 10–99.

This objective has behavior. It also has content. Copy the content portion by Number 9 on your answer sheet.

You should have copied:

> two-column addition problems in which the integers range from 10–99

Notice that the content of this objective is carefully described. Yet it is not limited to one single test item. A student who achieved this objective would be expected to generalize his ability to the entire set of two-digit integers 10–99. The universe, the entirety of the content relevant to the skill, could be sampled simply by using different problems. However, the statement was very economically written. Each possible pair was not listed, but rather a rule by which content could be selected was stated.

two-digit integers 10–99

Such an objective, while still behavioral, would be suitable for a period of time longer than a single lesson.

Let's take another case. For the next objective, designed for a first-grade child, decide whether the objective contains a rule limiting a universe of content or whether it is equivalent to a test item. Circle A for content rule or B for test item next to Number 10 on your answer sheet.

10.
To read the word "rate" aloud.

You should have marked B, since the response applies to a single bit of content and thus is equivalent to a single test item. How could this objective be rewritten so that a universe of content would be delimited? Answer by Number 11.

To read aloud words spelled in the consonant-vowel-consonant-silent e pattern.

This objective pairs a *set* of content with the specific behavior of reading aloud. All of the words to be read are described concisely. Not only would the original word be appropriate but many other words as well.

cope space cake fate rude joke pipe trite

If an objective is exactly equivalent to a test item, would that objective have content generality? Answer Yes or No by Number 12.

The answer is No. If a teacher's objective can be tested by only one particular item, then the objective does not have content generality.

For practice, judge which of the pairs of objectives has content generality, that is, which asks for behavior applied to more than a single specific test item. Circle your answer next to Number 13.

13.

A. TO BE ABLE TO DEMONSTRATE HOW TO DO A CARTWHEEL.

B. TO BE ABLE TO DEMONSTRATE ANY OF 5 BASIC WARM-UP EXERCISES.

The correct answer is B, since the student could demonstrate any of five exercises and not just one. Notice that both objectives call for behavior.

Circle A or B next to Number 14 for the objective which has content generality.

14.
A. To be able to state in writing the conflict in *Moby Dick.*
B. To be able to define the tone of any eighteenth-century Gothic novel.

Again, the correct answer is B. Both objectives contain student behavior, but objective A applies to one bit of content.

By Number 15, circle A or B for the objective which has content generality.

15.
A. To write a proof of any theorem in plane geometry.
B. To write the proof for the Pythagorean theorem.

You should have marked A, since the range of content to which the behavior can apply is wide.

You may note that there are varying degrees of precision with which content can be described beyond that limited to a single test item. You could say "all of Shelley's lyrics," "all of Shelley's poems," "all poems by writers in the Romantic tradition," "all English poems," and so on. Where possible, *rules* for selecting the content to which the behavior applies should be stated, such as those which can describe classes of mathematics problems to solve, or types of chemical bonds to graph where such precision is impossible. The rule defining the limits of content should be just as rigorous as you can make it.

OBJECTIVE ═ TEST ITEM

Try to convert this next objective into one in which content generality rather than test item equivalence is used. Write your answer next to Number 16.

16.
To list the economic effects of acquiring the Louisiana Purchase.

An appropriate answer might read:

> To list the economic effects of any territorial expansion of the United States prior to 1900.

For such an objective, many of the factors associated with the different expansions in United States history might be described. Different questions can be substituted, and the students can respond to the acquisition of Texas, Alaska, Cuba, and so on. The objective is stated, however, in a precise, economical way. Notice that the objective is still behavioral, but the content is much broadened.

For this next objective, substitute content generality for test item equivalence. Answer next to Number 17.

17.
To be able to use "slow" and "slowly" in sentences.

One modification of the objective so that content generality is operating is the following:

> The student will be able to use adjectives and adverbs in appropriate positions in written sentences.

The objective, again, remains operational. The content is radically expanded, from a consideration of "slow" and "slowly" to all adjectives and adverbs. Notice that objectives with content generality seem to be more suited for extended instructional periods.

Here is another opportunity for you to write an objective with content generality. Change this objective from a test item equivalence and write your answer by Number 18.

18.
To be able to write a budget for a family of four with an income of $8000 annually.

An acceptable modification might be this objective:

> To be able to write a budget for a family of from 2–8
> members with a yearly income ranging from $5000 to
> $14,000.

You should now be able to write objectives which define
broader sections of content than those usually associated
with behavioral objectives. Practice in writing such objectives
is obviously most relevant in your own subject matter area.

We have been arguing for content generality so far because
it is an economical way to proceed with preparing objectives.
You do not have to list every speck of content you intend to
teach but rather pair the intended behaviors with relatively
precise descriptions of the content domain. Precision and
behavioral objectives remain extremely important.

When a teacher realizes that students will usually learn what
they are taught and that other learnings are too erratic to
count on, he is faced squarely with the problem of justifying
the value of his objectives. There may be only trivial reasons
why anyone should learn to list three specific causes of
World War I. Aside from amassing information to dazzle
friends and acquaintances at social gatherings, the utility of
this particular response is highly questionable. If a teacher
could, however, define the larger class of content to which
the skill is intended to apply and, moreover, could teach the
students this application, he would rarely have to worry about
defending his objectives. The teacher might be able to
change his objectives so that the student would be able to
determine and state probable causes of any major conflict
between nations.

For reasons of economy, as well as important issues of the
justification of those objectives in which we wish to invest
our time, the use of content generality is advocated. Operational goals which have content generality make the writing
of behavioral objectives a feasible and rational endeavor
rather than an exhausting and perhaps unproductive exercise.

Writing Tests Which Measure Objectives

Objectives

This program is designed to help writers of objectives understand a useful procedure for the generation of test items to measure the objective. The program synthesizes information on the writing of objectives and includes dimensions not usually considered. At the conclusion of the program the learner should be able to:

1. Generate a list and brief description of each dimension of an item form.
2. Inspect an item generated from a set of item form specifications and indicate where any deviation in the item occurs.
3. Given an item form, generate an item which adheres to the specifications.

The topic of measurable objectives provokes polarized, stereotyped responses from most educators. One group insists that objectives represent *the* solution to a variety of problems, such as underfinancing of school programs, poor teaching, intransigent students, and, in California, earthquake damage. Their opposites display an equally predictable posture, portending that the adoption of objectives will stamp

MEASURABLE OBJECTIVES

out creativity (which flourishes so widely at the present time), turn students and teachers into automatons, bring the industrial-military complex into the classroom, and otherwise endanger the lives and longings of the American young people and their teachers.

Whether you side with one faction or with the other, you are sure to be wrong. The use of objectives can clearly not accomplish any of the outcomes described. However, even if you are moderate on the issue, you have not bettered your position by much. Objectives, by themselves, can do very little. Teachers can write objectives until their fingers are lumpy, school boards can decree the use of objectives by nailing parchment to school doors, and very little will change in the instructional programs.

The impotence of objectives alone has, in a diffuse way, begun to dawn on some of the people responsible for educational programs. Replacing previous incantations are newly formed rituals involving "evaluation systems" and "accountability." Their message, however, is important: the goals of instruction need to be evaluated. Possessing and proclaiming the use of instructional objectives means almost nothing until the results of the instructional programs are measured.

Although the idea of measuring instructional goals is certainly not dramatic, school people are currently stymied about how to proceed. However great the urge to evaluate, the means are currently limited to traditionally developed standardized tests. While such tests are carefully constructed and useful instruments for some purposes, they are designed to measure achievement in general terms rather than measure progress toward specifically stated objectives. Such general measures are not helpful in the evaluation of objectives because of the difficulty in obtaining information relevant to particular objectives. Schools learn whether their students are deficient in an area, such as mathematical concepts, without learning which concepts need additional (not a pun) work. Thus, many school administrators display particular symptoms of schizophrenia: they insist on clearly stated instructional objectives which precisely describe learner achievement while at the same time they require the use of general measures for the evaluation of school programs.

Into the confusion enters the topic of criterion-referenced measurement, which holds that objectives should be measured by items relevant to them. Since objectives-based tests are not widely available at the present time, the necessity for their local construction is clear.

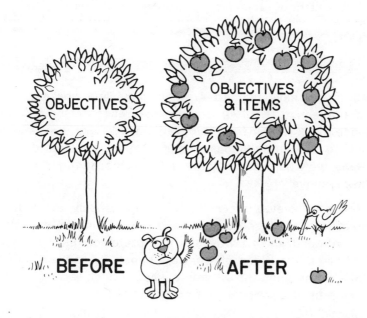

How can you construct objectives-based tests? If you bring to the task habits from previous test construction attempts, the products of your efforts are likely to be poor. Items should not, for instance, "seem" to be relevant to the objectives. They must sample directly the behaviors and content described in the objectives if they are to improve the information gained from these tests as opposed to standardized achievement tests.

Certain dimensions should be present in the items to demonstrate their relationship to the objectives on logical grounds. Ideally, the demonstration should be empirical. How would you expect a student to perform on items related to a single objective? Circle A or B by Number 1 on your answer sheet.

1.
A. He should probably get most of them right, or most of them wrong.
B. His pattern of scoring is not predictable.

You should have marked A. If all items are measuring the same objective, then we would expect each person's performance to be similar from item to item. We would expect the items to be homogeneous. If performance on items differed greatly, we would expect that the test is measuring more than one objective.

In order to develop items which homogeneously test a single objective, certain sources of variation in performance must be controlled. In this way, the interpreter of testing results will have a good idea of what the capability of the students is at a given point and what implications such testing has for revision of instructional programs.

A plan for the preparation of test items must take account of all dimensions which the curriculum planner deems important. Plans for writing such items, called "item forms," were originally developed by Wells Hively and his associates at the University of Minneapolis. Although Dr. Hively had a different purpose in mind, the major attributes of his methodology can be applied to the problem of writing test items which homogeneously measure specific objectives.

During this program, you will be introduced to the preparation of item forms for instructional objectives. Hopefully, you will value the procedure so that writing objectives alone will not continue to be in your repertoire, if it ever was. Instead you will write complete item forms. If you are supervising the production of tests, item forms provide you with an organized procedure to review items. Item forms, in simplified version, have six major attributes. Each controls an important dimension of performance and scoring so that results derived from item form-based tests are readily interpretable. The six attributes are:

1. Response description
2. Content limits
3. Item format
4. Criteria
5. Test directions
6. Sample test item

The first attribute of an item form is the *response description.* Response descriptions are easily extrapolated from instructional objectives which are operationally written. For instance, in the following objective, figure out the response description. Write your answer by Number 2 on your answer sheet.

2.
Given a set of statistics, the student will construct a graph.

You should have written the section " ... construct a graph," for that section tells exactly what the student is to be doing.

Decide the response description in the next objective. Write your answer by Number 3 on your answer sheet.

3.
Given a series of short stories, the student will identify and write a one-sentence statement of the theme.

You should have written "... identify and write a one-sentence statement of the theme," the section which specified the learner activity.

It is important in preparing a test to be sure that response descriptions are specified, for in this way an important source of student performance begins to be controlled. If the form of the response is allowed to vary, for instance, if students can "identify" short story themes in multiple choice tests as well as write them, differences in learner performance are to be expected. If you seriously wish to find out whether students can select themes as well as write one-sentence statements of them, then you need to prepare a separate item form for theme selection. Response description is an obvious attribute, derived from what is commonly thought of as the "behavioral" section of the objective.

The second attribute of an item form is far more difficult: *content limits* for the objective must be described. If specific objectives have any importance, it is that they specify a domain of competence which the student possesses. For instance, solving $36 \times 12 = ?$ is not significant in itself. A series of ten such items, however, begins to sample the student's ability to solve problems of a given complexity in a *transfer* or nonschool situation. Writing content limits helps you clarify the domain of *transfer* you feel is important. In the example, "To read words in a consonant-vowel-consonant-e pattern," the content limits are partially provided, for any item would be acceptable if it conformed to the above requirements, that is, if it was constructed in c-v-c-e pattern. The words "make," "home," "rude," and "white" would all conform to the rule.

Thus content limits should be thought of as the *rule* you use to select contents for objectives, and therefore, for test items. The rule *limits* the content which you think the student should be able to work with. Attempting to write a rule may also show you that you have grossly underestimated the subject matter.

In addition, the act of specifying content limits in effect pro-
hibits you from using single instances as content for objectives—certain people have written poor objectives such as,
"The student can hum 'Yankee Doodle.'" Without arguing the
merit of the particular tune, it is clear that such an objective
specifies no transfer domain. Teaching children to hum "Yankee Doodle" can be boring. An objective written in item form

would include dimensions of melodies such as "Yankee Doodle" as simple 4/4 measure, one octave range, and so on, so
that Yankee Doodle might represent only a single sample of
a defined set of tunes the child could hum. If the procedure
sounds too complicated, then probably you didn't really want
Yankee Doodle-humming as an objective. Sometimes favorite
activities get labeled as objectives because that seems an
easy thing to do. Trying to write content limits for such objectives quickly enables you to discern which goals are worth
the trouble. If they are important enough to warrant the writ-

ing of objectives, then they are important enough for proper test items to be constructed for them, too. The content limits of an item, then, should define the set of content to which the objective is relevant. If that set can be proscribed by a rule, such as the earlier spelling pattern example, the attribute of item forms is easily satisfied. Sometimes it is difficult or impractical to formulate the rule to describe the relevant content. A rule such as "all twentieth-century narrative poetry" represents a fake content domain, for it is too broad to be practically manageable. Further, the differences among individual twentieth-century narrative poems are so great that there is little reason to believe instruction on a sample of them will transfer to another sample of poems. Instead it may be more reasonable to specify the *actual set* of poems which will be used in instruction. Suppose the objective were that the student were to be able to identify and describe the forms of government in particular European countries. The content limits might look like the following:

> *Content Limits:* Countries included in the objective: France, Portugal, Italy, Denmark, Germany (West), the Netherlands.

In this example the set of content was spelled out. It was more a practical procedure than generating a rule. However, when the set of content becomes very large, it is more economical to attempt to formulate a rule to describe the content. But be sure that the content limits indicate the range of content expected to be learned.

For the following example, circle Yes or No by Number 4 on your answer sheet to indicate whether the content limits provided are satisfactory.

4.

Response description: To be able to solve simple equations.
Content limits: No more than one unknown; no fractional values; not more than three expressions in each equation.

The answer is Yes. Rules are provided for the selection of appropriate equations to be included in the items.

Are the content limits in this next example satisfactory? Answer by Number 5 on your answer sheet.

5.
Response description: To read a story and answer factual questions.
Content limits: Stories are found in text distributed.

The content limits provided were not satisfactory, so you should have marked No. The set of stories was not clearly specified (and probably not for any better reason than their availability in a text), but the real problem was that the nature of the factual questions was unclear. What kinds of questions need to be clearly described?

Satisfactory content limits should provide a rule for the selection of content which describes the range of the content the students will learn or a particularized listing of content. In either case, the specification of content limits will inevitably make the objective or item writer much more judicious in his selection of content for objectives. The delineation of rules or the display of content has a way of betraying some of our less well formulated plans. Writing content limits will probably reduce the number of objectives you plan to implement, but should drastically raise the general quality of the ones you select.

The third dimension of item forms which needs attention, in addition to response description and content limits, is the *item format.* The item format merely elaborates further the information provided in the response description. For instance, if the response description read, "From a series of excerpts the learner was to select those which illustrated the alienation theme in America," it would be important to understand exactly how the items were going to be prepared. Items could measure the objective by having the learner circle those in a list which related to the alienation theme; they might be arrayed in multiple choice format with two, three, or four wrong answers. The difficulty inherent in those two tasks is quite different. If item format were not specified, then an important source of variation could be introduced into the testing situation.

A fourth essential element of item form production is the inclusion of the *criteria,* or standards, the responses must meet. This is always a tricky problem for constructed responses, where the learner produces or prepares an answer rather than selecting one from an array provided by the item writer. The criteria should describe statements of what the answer must include to be considered satisfactory. For instance, if the response description called for the learner to prepare an analysis of the merits of scientific experiment, what should the learner do to assure that his answer will be judged appropriate? One easily thought-of criterion relates to the length of the paper. Many times we encounter objectives where a 500 word length is provided as the criterion. Such a criterion borders on the absurd, unless the teacher wants to test sustained small motor control. It certainly isn't sufficient for distinguishing between good and poor responses—all 500 word papers pass and those of fewer words fail. The best way to generate the criteria for constructed responses is to look at the subobjectives of any task. For instance, before a student could properly critique a scientific experiment, he or she would have to be able to identify a manipulated variable, and he would have to identify the dependent measure, that is, how the effects were to be assessed. To prepare a proper analysis, all of the above points, and probably more, would need to be considered. The criteria section of the item form would read:

Criteria:
A. Identifies manipulated variable.
B. Identifies experimental controls.
C. Identifies dependent measure.

Students who omitted any of these points would not have satisfactorily completed the assignment. The delineation of specific criteria also provides clear data for revision purposes. If, for instance, many students omitted the identification of experimental controls, the teacher or designer of the instructional program would have some idea about what particular section of the learning experience needed revision. The use of a criterion such as 500 words in length doesn't supply the instructional designer with much useful information for revision of the instructional sequence.

The provision of criteria for constructed responses is placed importantly in most published discussions of the preparation of instructional goals. It is included on the item form so that the reviewer is informed of the scoring procedures planned. A different and more complex problem is presented if you wish to extrapolate the criterion problem to selected responses. The question is still essentially the same: What should the students be able to display to indicate mastery? The common solution to this question is to provide a number, such as 90 percent of the items or some other equally arbitrary figure. But that does not adequately answer the question. Think of a series of multiple choice test questions, where the response description calls for the students to identify sentences which contain imagery. If the item format described a four-option multiple choice question, the critical question to answer in writing the items involves the description of both what the right and what the wrong answers will be. Suppose we determine that the right answers will include the use of metaphor and simile. How are the alternatives which surround the correct answers to be written? If we follow usual practice, we write the correct answer, then think of a plausible alternative, a slightly more peculiar alternative, and then one that is quite wrong, far out from the range of reasonable answers. If each of a series of items is written in this way, we have an idea that the learner can select correct answers, but we have no understanding of what he is selecting them from. Further, if the learners do not perform well on the test, we have almost no information to assist in revision.

When item formats call for selected responses, as in multiple choice or true-false situations, the item writer must clearly describe the population of wrong answers. For instance, in

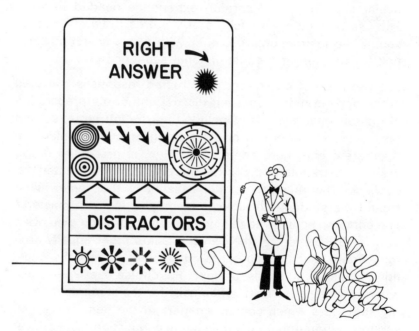

the example with imagery, wrong answers might consist of sentences with descriptive adjectives in them. In that way, students would be more seriously challenged than if they were choosing the examples of imagery from sentences such as "The dog barked and barked." It is a shocking experience to attempt to write a description of those alternatives which will constitute wrong answers. In some ways, it is similar to the specification of content limits. Without the procedure, the understanding you have of the student's ability is greatly impaired.

The fifth check point on the use of the item form is labeled *test directions.* The item writer needs to prepare a sample of the directions to accompany the item format. The provision of test directions allows the reviewer of the item form to determine whether the directions are calling for the same kind of responses indicated in the response description and item format statements. Very slight shifts in the wording of the directions can produce markedly different responses. Sometimes the writer of directions gets "cute" at the last minute, adds a sentence or two, and radically changes the behavior the learner is to display. For example, assume that the response description asks the learner to identify the theme of a short story, and the item format calls for a short written answer. Would directions which looked like the following be appropriate? Circle Yes or No by Number 6 on your answer sheet.

6.
Directions: Read the short story provided. Then write a brief statement of the theme and how it relates to any one of the author's previous works.

The directions as provided are not appropriate to the response description for they require an additional task of the learner: stating the relationship of the theme to previous works. In the next example see if the directions match the statement of the response description and item format. Assume that the response description calls for the learner to find the sums of pairs of two-digit integers. The item format requires the learner to construct his answer. Circle Yes by Number 7 on your answer sheet if the directions are appropriate. If they are not, circle No and indicate in a phrase what is wrong with them.

7.

Directions: Look at the following completed addition problem. If it is correct, check it. If it is wrong, correct it.

This is slightly more interesting than the previous example, for to satisfy the requirements stated in the directions, the respondent has to compute the answer to the problem. However, he has to compare his answer with the provided answer, which is a separate, but probably trivial, task. He is also being provided with substantial assistance because the test writers will likely provide wrong answers which closely approximate the correct one. The answer to $42 + 77$ is not likely to be given as 6. Thus, the learner will be naturally encouraged to be more careful in computation than he ordinarily might. The behavior actually obtained in response to the directions is considerably different than providing learners with problems and telling them to find the sums. The answer to Number 7, we believe, should have been No.

For the next example, see if the directions match the responses described in the response description and item format statements. Mark your answer sheet by Number 8.

8.

Response description: To produce sketch which uses shading to give a three-dimensional effect.
Item format: Constructed response, presenting necessary materials.
Directions: From the objects on the table, select one to draw. Try to present a full and rounded rendering of the object so that your sketch has depth.

These directions appear to conform to the item format and response description statements provided. Notice that the directions do not use the exact language of the response description. The term "three-dimensional" is not used in the directions. But the essential requirements of the response are preserved.

The sixth and final step in the preparation of an item form to measure an instructional objective is to include a *sample test item* which conforms to the requirement as presented in the objective. The sample item is particularly important if the item form is being prepared to guide others in the preparation of item pools. The presentation of a concrete example of all the requirements is indispensible; obviously, it is not sufficient because the specification of the response description, content limits, item form, and criteria provide helpful information which enables the item writer to be likely to produce test items which relate to each other along identifiable dimensions. The elements of the item form again are as follows:

1. Response description
2. Content limits
3. Item format
4. Criteria
5. Test directions
6. Sample test item

The next exercise should help you check your understanding of the item form approach to test item production. You will be presented with an item form and a sample item. Indicate whether the item conforms to the requirements stated in the item form. If it does not, circle the elements which are at variance with the item. Answer by Number 9 on your answer sheet.

9.

Response description: To form new words by adding suffixes.

Content limits: Suffix to be included: "-tion"; words to be simple verbs and nouns of not more than two syllables.

Item format: Presented with a word and a suffix, to write a new word.

Criteria: Words formed must be composed of elements presented; they must be spelled correctly.

Item:

Directions: Here is a series of words. Add "-tion."

emote   attend   resolve   rotate

The items here generally conform to the limits established in the item form. You may have had some problem with both "attend" and "resolve" because more was required than a simple transformation of dropping the "e" and adding "-tion." Notice that the item format states that the learner will be presented with one word at a time, whereas the item presents a multiple word task. To be absolutely correct, you should have checked the item format space on your answer sheet.

Try this next item:

10.

Response description: To be able to identify physical features on a map.

Content limits: Maps will not include political features; elevation, vegetation, and waterways will be included with a range in their height, density, and length, respectively.

Item format: Presented with a map of a country, to identify the point of greatest elevation, the longest waterway, the most dense vegetation by drawing a line to the appropriate features.

Criteria: Only the single correct answer for each feature should be indicated.

Item directions: Draw a line which indicates the highest point on the map; draw a dotted line to the longest waterway; draw a broken line to the area of densest vegetation.

The item generally conforms to the limitations of the item form. Although the item format specifies only that a "line should be drawn," and the item calls for broken and dotted lines, only a superpurist would call the item not relevant to the requirements.

Here is an opportunity for you to try your hand at the complex task of producing an item form. The subject matter presented will be simple so that you will need no specialized information. Try to complete the portions of the item form presented. Write your answer by Number 11.

11.

Response description: To find the perimeter of a simple geometric figure.

Content limits: Squares, rectangles, equilateral triangles (one side given in the case of squares and triangles, and adjacent sides in the rectangles).

Item format:

Criteria:

Directions:

Sample item:

You might have handled this problem in a number of ways but here is one version of the completed item form sections:

> *Item format:* One geometric figure should be presented in each item. Students should fill in their answer in space provided.
> *Criteria:* Answers must be accurately computed. Students should label all sides of the figure.
> *Directions:* Find the perimeter of this figure. Label each side and fill in the answer in the space provided.

Try this next example. Answer by Number 12 on your answer sheet.

12.

Response description: Given a series of different graphs, to circle the graph depicting the highest value of a variable.

Item format: Multiple choice: the student is presented with three graphs and must circle the graph with the highest value of a given variable.

Content limits:

Criteria:

Directions:

Sample item:

You might have substituted the following elements into the item form.

> *Content limits:* Circle, bar, and line graphs will be used. They will be oriented both vertically and horizontally. Labels for variables will reflect common commodities, e.g., corn, wheat. Graph scale will vary.
>
> *Criteria:* (for wrong answers) At least one answer will be within five units of the correct value. At least one answer will be drawn to another scale.
>
> *Directions:* From the graphs presented below, circle the one with the highest production of corn.
>
> *Sample item:*

SAMPLE ITEM

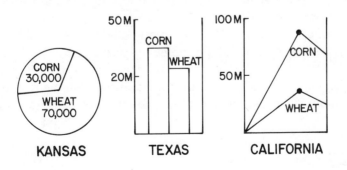

KANSAS   TEXAS   CALIFORNIA

This program has been designed to introduce you to the notion of writing item forms. The exercises give you some idea of the complexity of thought which should go into the production of even the most simple set of test items. You certainly will need additional practice in trying to use the item form procedure in subject matter areas of personal interest. Hopefully you will recognize that the production of homogeneous test items is merely approximated by the use of the item form and the examples presented here have been especially simplified for purposes of example.

The final message, however, is identical with the original one: don't write objectives if you aren't going to write test items to measure them. The item form approach may help you to write items which can give you good information about your instructional programs. If you don't want to take the trouble, then don't waste your time with objectives. For those of you with doubts, select a single objective and attempt to develop one or more item forms for it. Have the item form critiqued by colleagues and then try to develop some test items from it. If you actually give the items to students, you will get better information regarding how the item form statement might be revised. Just like everything else, item forms won't by themselves change the flow of American education. But they might allow you to obtain better information about what you're doing.

Program
Answer
Sheets

Humanizing Educational Objectives *Answer Sheet*

1. _____

2. _____

3. _____
   _____
   _____

4. Needs Assessment
   1. _____
   2. _____
   3. _____
      A. _____
      B. _____
      C. _____

5. _____
   _____
   _____

6. Needs Assessment
   1. _____
   2. _____
   3. _____
      A. _____
      B. _____
      C. _____

7. Implementation
   1. _____
   2. _____

Deciding on Defensible Goals Via Educational Needs Assessment *Answer Sheet*

1. _____
   _____
   _____
   _____

2. _____
   _____
   _____

3. Circle one: 5   4   3   2   1
                (5 = very important, 1 = very unimportant)

4. Objective number ____

5. Different weightings? Yes ____ No ____; If so, which group?
   _____

6. A ____   B ____

7. Yes ____   No ____

8. A: ____%   B: ____%

9. _____
   _____
   _____

10. 1   2   3   4   5

Identifying Affective Objectives *Answer Sheet*

1. (C = Cognitive, A = Affective, P = Psychomotor)
   A _____
   B _____
   C _____
2. A _____
   B _____
   C _____
   D _____
   E _____
3. Yes _____   No _____
4. A _____   B _____
5. A _____   B _____
6. (1) _____

   _____

   (2) _____

   _____

   (3) _____

   _____

   (4) _____

   _____

7. _____

   _____

8. _____

   _____

9. (1) _____

   _____

   (2) _____

   _____

   (3) _____

   _____

Classroom Instructional Tactics

Evaluating Instruction

Expanding Dimensions of Instructional Objectives

W. James Popham

Eva L. Baker

PRENTICE-HALL, INC.
Englewood Cliffs, New Jersey

Defining Content for Objectives *Answer Sheet*

1. A   B
2. A   B
3. _____
4. _____
5. _____
6. Yes   No
7. Yes   No
8. Yes   No
9. _____
10. A   B
11. _____
12. Yes   No
13. A   B
14. A   B
15. A   B
16. _____
    _____
17. _____
    _____
18. _____
    _____

Writing Tests Which Measure Objectives *Answer Sheet*

1. A   B
2. _____
3. _____
4. Yes   No
5. Yes   No
6. Yes   No
7. Yes   No
8. Yes   No
9. *Response description:* To form new words by adding
    suffixes.
    Content limits: Suffix to be included: "-tion"; words to be
        simple verbs and nouns of not more than two syllables.
    Item format: Presented with a word and a suffix, to write the
        new word.
    Criteria: Words formed must be composed of elements pre-
        sented; they must be spelled correctly.
    Item:
    Directions: Here is a series of words. Add "-tion."
    emote   attend   resolve   rotate
    Yes   No
    response description _____
    content limits _____
    item format _____
    criteria _____
    test directions _____
10. *Response description:* To be able to identify physical fea-
        tures on a map.
    Content limits: Maps will not include political features; eleva-
        tion, vegetation, and waterways will be included with a
        range in their height, density, and length, respectively.
    Item format: Presented with a map of a country, to identify
        the point of greatest elevation, the longest waterway, the
        most dense vegetation by drawing a line to the appropri-
        ate features.
    Criteria: Only the single correct answer for each feature
        should be indicated.
    Test directions: Draw a line which indicates the highest point
        on the map; draw a dotted line to the longest waterway;
        draw a broken line to the area of densest vegetation.

Yes   No
response description _____
content limits _____
item format _____
criteria _____
test directions _____

11. *Response description:* To find the perimeter of a simple geometric figure.

Content limits: Squares, rectangles, equilateral triangles (one
side given in the case of squares and triangles, and adjacent sides in the rectangles).

Item format:

Criteria:

Directions:

Sample item: ⌷⌷⌷⌷⌷   3

7

12. *Response description:* Given a series of different graphs, to
circle the graph depicting the highest value of a variable.

Item format: Multiple choice: the student is presented with
three graphs and must circle the graph with the highest
value of a given variable.

Content limits:

Criteria:

Test directions:

Sample item:

Mastery
Tests

Mastery Test: Humanizing Educational Objectives

Name_____

1. Write an objective which deals in process.

   _____

   _____

2. Describe the steps in using student-based needs assessment.

   1. _____

   2. _____

   3. _____

      a. _____

      b. _____

      c. _____

3. Describe two ways to implement objectives to make them appropriate to students' needs.

   1. _____

   2. _____

Mastery Test: Deciding on Defensible Goals Via Educational Needs Assessment

Name_____

Imagine that you are the department chairman of a group of fifteen social science teachers in a junior high school, grades 7–9. Your faculty wishes to conduct an educational needs assessment in order to decide on four or five high priority social science goals for the academic year and have asked you to describe the major elements of a needs assessment plan which they can use. In the space provided below, and on the reverse, if necessary, in *no more than fifteen minutes* write a first draft of such a plan which you might present to them.

(When using this test locally, type the above paragraph at the top of an 8½ by 11 inch sheet.)

Mastery Test: Identifying Affective Objectives

Name_____

Part I.

1. Describe a strategy for identifying instructional objectives in the affective domain.

   For each general nonbehavioral objective, write out as many behaviorally stated affective objectives as you can. *Number each objective,* please. (Test constructor should choose one of these for pretest and a different one for posttest.)

Part II.

2. For this general nonbehavioral objective, write out as many behaviorally stated affective objectives as you can. *Number each objective, please.* (Test constructor should choose one of these for pretest and a different one for posttest.)

   The student will become interested in art.
   The student will develop a positive attitude toward the democratic process.
   The student will display the qualities of a good citizen.
   The student will wish to continue his education beyond the 12th grade.
   The student will enjoy sports as a participant or a spectator.
   The student will display good sportsmanship.

Mastery Test: Defining Content for Objectives

Name_____

Part I.

1. Briefly describe the relationship an objective should have to a test item.

Part II. *Directions:* Indicate which of the following objectives possess content generality by placing an X in the place provided.

_____ 2. To be able to drive any automatic transmission car.

_____ 3. To be able to recite the "Pledge of Allegiance."

_____ 4. To be able to describe in an essay the effects of the Point Four Program in postwar Europe.

_____ 5. To be able to write a summary of any nineteenth-century English narrative poem.

_____ 6. To be able to write the alphabet in cursive script.

_____ 7. To be able to solve the equation $7 + 3X + 2Y = 16 - 2X$.

_____ 8. To be able to describe the three motives described in class for Hamlet's behavior.

Part III. *Directions:* Change the following objectives so that they possess content generality.

9. To be able to draw a triangle.

_____

10. To be able to underline the segments of the 1972 Democratic platform statement in which emotional appeal is used.

_____
_____
_____

Mastery Test: Writing Tests Which Measure Objectives

Name_____

1. List and briefly describe the six dimensions of a complete item form.

   1. _____

   2. _____

   3. _____

   4. _____

   5. _____

   6. _____

> For the following section, read the item form carefully. Then look at the sample item provided. Indicate whether the item conforms to the specifications of the item form. If it does not conform, check the dimensions where it deviates.

2. *Item form*
   Response description: To substitute noun clauses for nouns.
   Content limits: Noun clauses considered are those employed as subject. Basic declarative sentence patterns should be used. Complement (direct object) and object of preposition.
   Item format: Short answer, with sentence for substitution underlined.
   Criteria: Substitution produced by student must be a noun clause. Its position in sentence should conform to directions.
   Directions: Substitute in the following sentences a noun clause for the noun.
   Item: I bought a *jacket.*

Does the item conform to the description in the item form? If not, check the dimensions where it varies.

Yes_____ No_____

response description _____

content limits _____

item format _____

criteria _____

directions _____

3. *Item form*

   Response description: To subtract numbers.

   Content limits: Two-digit integers.

   Item format: When presented with a problem in which the pairs of numbers are vertically arrayed, to write the correct answer in the space provided.

   Criteria: Answers need to be computationally accurate. Erasures are permitted. Carrying does not need to be demonstrated.

   Directions: Subtract these numbers and write your answer in the space provided.

   Item: 45–17 = _____;
$$\begin{array}{r} 324 \\ -\ 10 \\ \hline \end{array}$$

Does the item conform to the item form? If not, check the dimensions where it varies.

Yes_____ No_____

response description _____

content limits _____

item format _____

criteria _____

directions _____

     Generate an item with directions which conforms to the following specifications:

4. *Item form*

   Response description: To use the same word as different parts of speech (form classes).

   Content limits: Words will be used as nouns, adverbs, adjectives, verbs.

   Item format: The learner is provided a word and directions to use it in at least two separate sentences as a different part of speech. Part of speech desired is indicated.

   Sample item (with directions): Use the word *game* in two sentences as a noun and as a verb.

     Write your item here:

Answers to
Mastery
Tests

Humanizing Educational Objectives

1. An observable behavior which deals in a social or personal attribute.
2. (1) Teacher explains purpose of the needs assessment.
    (2) Students and teacher cooperatively develop set of objectives.
    (3) Develop priorities among objectives by:
        (A) Preparing and administering questionnaire on interest and importance.
        (B) Pretesting students to find out present performance.
        (C) Make judgment based on information.
3. (1) Different objectives for different students.
    (2) Tell students the objectives.

Deciding on Defensible Goals
Via Educational Needs Assessment

A possible scoring scheme when used as a Pretest and Posttest:
Take a random sample of pretest and posttest responses, equal numbers of each, then code them so that you, but not the reviewing judge, can discern which were completed before or after the program. Then mix the responses and give a judge (or judges) with a charge such as: "Sort these papers into two *equal* piles, inferior and superior, based on your general estimate of the degree to which their implementation would yield the selection of defensible educational goals." After the split has been made, the proportion of posttest responses assigned to the superior category can be identified. Hopefully, of course, the proportion of posttest responses in the superior category will markedly exceed the proportion of posttest responses designated as inferior.

Identifying Affective Objectives

Part I.
1. (Answers correct if congruent with four-step strategy described in program.)
    1. Imagine an individual who possesses the affective attribute.
    2. Imagine an individual who does not possess the affective attribute.

3. Generate situations where the two hypothetical individuals would behave differently.
4. Select objectives from such situations.

Part II.

2. (Test coordinator should count number of objectives student produces on pretest and posttest.)
   1. The student will become interested in art.
   2. The student will develop a positive attitude toward the democratic process.
   3. The student will display the qualities of a good citizen.
   4. The student will wish to continue his education beyond the twelfth grade.
   5. The student will enjoy sports as a participant or as a spectator.
   6. The student will display good sportsmanship.

Defining Content for Objectives

Part I.

1. An objective should usually define a *class* of test items and generally not be equivalent to a single item.

Part II.

2. ___X___
3. _____
4. _____
5. ___X___
6. _____
7. _____
8. _____

Part III.

9. To be able to draw any geometric figure.
10. To be able to underline segments of any political statement in which emotional appeal is used.

Writing Tests Which Measure Objectives

1. (1) Response description
   (2) Content limits
   (3) Item format

(4) Criteria
(5) Test directions
(6) Sample test item

2. Yes ____X____   No _____
    response description _____
    content limits _____
    item format _____
    criteria _____
    directions _____

3. Yes _____   No ____X____
    response description _____
    content limits _____
    item format ____X____
    criteria _____
    directions _____

4. Satisfactory items might model the following:
    Use the word "front" in two separate sentences as a noun
    and as an adjective.